THE BEST MATCHES OF WORLD SOCCER

BY LUKE HANLON

SportsZone

An Imprint of Abdo Publishing
abdobooks.com

abdobooks.com

Published by Abdo Publishing, a division of ABDO, PO Box 398166, Minneapolis, Minnesota 55439. Copyright © 2024 by Abdo Consulting Group, Inc. International copyrights reserved in all countries. No part of this book may be reproduced in any form without written permission from the publisher. SportsZone™ is a trademark and logo of Abdo Publishing.

Printed in the United States of America, North Mankato, Minnesota.
102023
012024

Cover Photo: Peter Robinson/EMPICS/PA Images/Getty Images (left); PA Images/Getty Images (middle); Laurence Griffiths/FIFA/Getty Images (right)
Interior Photos: ullstein bild/Getty Images, 4–5; AFP/Getty Images, 6, 8, 16, 40; Jon Buckle/EMPICS/PA Images/Getty Images, 9; Roberto Schmidt/AFP/Getty Images, 10; Ben Radford/Getty Images Sport/Getty Images, 13; EMPICS Sport/PA Images/Getty Images, 14–15; dpa/picture alliance/Getty Images, 19; David Cannon/Allsport/David Cannon Collection/Getty Images, 20; John MacDougall/AFP/Getty Images, 23; Daniel Roland/AFP/Getty Images, 25; Etsuo Hara/Getty Images Sport/Getty Images, 26–27, 28; Robert Michael/AFP/Getty Images, 30; Ed Garvey/Manchester City FC/Getty Images, 32; Wally Skalij/Los Angeles Times/Getty Images, 35; PA Images/Getty Images, 36–37, 38; Stuart Franklin/FIFA/Getty Images, 41; Michael Regan/FIFA/Getty Images, 43; Julian Finney/Getty Images Sport/Getty Images, 45

Editor: Chrös McDougall
Series Designers: Karli Kruse and Joshua Olson

Library of Congress Control Number: 2023939431

Publisher's Cataloging-in-Publication Data

Names: Hanlon, Luke, author.
Title: The best matches of world soccer / by Luke Hanlon
Description: Minneapolis, Minnesota: Abdo Publishing, 2024 | Series: The best of world soccer | Includes online resources and index.
Identifiers: ISBN 9781098292263 (lib. bdg.) | ISBN 9798384910206 (ebook)
Subjects: LCSH: Soccer--Juvenile literature. | Professional sports--Juvenile literature. | Soccer matches--Juvenile literature. | Soccer Teams--Juvenile literature. | Soccer--Records--Juvenile literature.
Classification: DDC 796.334--dc23

TABLE OF CONTENTS

CHAPTER 1

CHAMPIONSHIP GLORY

Soccer, as we know it today, was founded in England during the mid-1800s. The sport began spreading around the world soon after. And in 1930, the first men's World Cup was held. Brazil was tapped to host the fourth World Cup, which was held in 1950. To mark the occasion, the country built

a grand new stadium in Rio de Janeiro. The massive Maracanã
was finished just eight days before the tournament began.

The final round of that tournament featured a four-team
group stage between Brazil, Uruguay, Sweden, and Spain. The
team with the best record against the other three opponents
would be the champion. After two games, Brazil had two wins.
Uruguay had a win and a draw. When the South American
neighbors faced each other on July 16, Brazil needed only to tie
the match to claim the country's first World Cup title.

Uruguay had won the first World Cup in 1930. But Brazil's
tiny neighbor was a huge underdog in the 1950 match. It didn't
help that a huge home crowd turned up for Brazil. The official
attendance for the match was 173,000. However, it is estimated
that more than 200,000 fans made their way into the Maracanã
that day.

The people of Brazil were full of confidence. Local
newspapers had already printed editions declaring the
Brazilians world champions. A band was set up on the sideline
to play after Brazil won. It was one large 90-minute party to
celebrate the country's first world title.

Through 79 minutes, the teams were deadlocked at 1–1.
The score wasn't ideal for Brazil, but it was enough. Then
Uruguayan midfielder Alcides Ghiggia sneaked down the right

wing and sent a low, hard shot on goal. When the ball slipped past Brazil goalkeeper Barbosa at his near post, the massive crowd turned silent. Tens of thousands of stunned Brazil fans could only watch as Uruguay went on to win 2–1 and claim its second World Cup title.

Though the Brazil–Uruguay match wasn't officially a final, it served as one because the result would determine the tournament champion. Today the World Cup final is more straightforward. Like most other tournaments, the World Cup uses a knockout format for the later rounds. It ends with the two remaining teams meeting for the title. Finals are pressure-packed matches. The result determines the champion. Players and fans remember these games for the rest of their lives. Naturally, some of the most iconic games in soccer history have come in such finals.

Uruguay's Juan Alberto Schiaffino scores in the 66th minute to put his team even with Brazil at 1–1 in the deciding game of the 1950 World Cup.

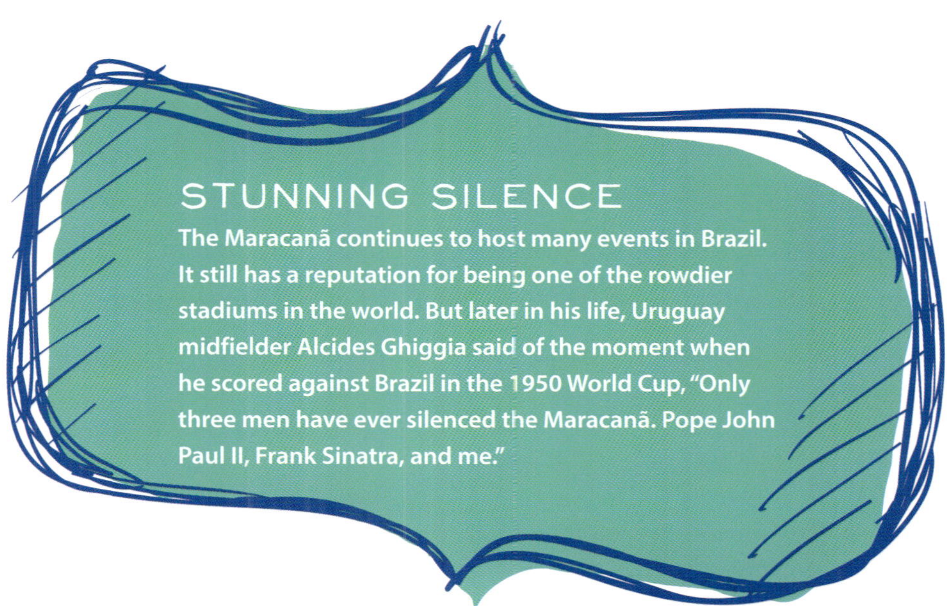

MARADONA CONQUERS THE WORLD

Argentina had the best player in the world on its side at the 1986 men's World Cup in Mexico. Attacking midfielder Diego Maradona stood only 5 feet, 5 inches tall, but he towered above the soccer world. *"El Pibe de Oro"*—"The Golden Boy"— had scored two spectacular goals in each of the quarterfinal and semifinal games. Now he led his team out against West Germany for the final at Mexico City's fabled Estadio Azteca. The soccer world wondered what he would do next.

Coming off a runner-up finish in 1982, West Germany had other ideas. The squad had not allowed a goal in three knockout games in 1986. To continue that streak in the final, the Germans stuck midfielder Lothar Matthäus on Maradona. The 25-year-old Matthäus shadowed the Argentine superstar around the field. And the plan worked—kind of. Matthäus was successful in slowing Maradona. However, Argentina teammates José Luis Brown and Jorge Valdano filled in. Both players scored, and the South Americans held a 2–0 lead early in the second half.

West Germany's Lothar Matthäus slides to try to stop Argentina superstar Diego Maradona during the 1986 World Cup final.

Then West Germany battled back. Captain Karl-Heinz Rummenigge scored off a corner kick in the 74th minute. Striker Rudi Völler tied things up eight minutes later.

Needing a spark, Argentina's superstar finally broke through. With five minutes left before stoppage time, Maradona collected the ball with some space just inside his own half. Several West German defenders closed in. But Maradona spotted teammate Jorge Burruchaga open ahead of him. He lobbed a pass into Burruchaga's path for a clean breakaway. The midfielder slipped the ball into the West German net for the deciding goal in a thrilling 3–2 win.

After the final, Maradona fell to his knees in celebration. He was then carried off the field on the shoulders of fans. It was the only World Cup the Argentine legend ever won. But it cemented his place among the sport's all-time great players.

HISTORY IN THE MAKING

The first Women's World Cup was played in 1991 in China. Few fans witnessed the United States' title-game victory over Norway. But the sport had come a long way by the 1999 final. The match was played at the massive Rose Bowl stadium in Pasadena, California. It drew a crowd of 90,185 fans, at the time a record for a women's soccer match.

Even though the US team was at home, many considered China the favorite. Its star, Sun Wen, had led the tournament with seven goals. But the United States had plenty of great players, too. Striker Mia Hamm,

China's Sun Wen races up the field with the ball against Norway in the 1999 Women's World Cup semifinals.

midfielders Julie Foudy and Michelle Akers, and defender Brandi Chastain were among the many superstars on the roster.

The teams played out a tense, scoreless tie through 90 minutes in the brutal Southern California heat. Akers, the veteran team leader, had to leave the game due to dehydration. Without her, the Americans barely survived the 30-minute extra time. Midfielder Kristine Lilly had to head a shot off the goal line to keep the game scoreless.

The game—and world championship—came down to a penalty shootout. Both teams scored on their first two shots. Then US goalkeeper Brianna Scurry lunged to her left to stop Liu Ying's attempt. The next four shooters all scored. That set up Chastain as the final shooter. If she scored, the United States would be champion again.

Chastain aimed her shot for the upper right-hand corner of the net. China goalkeeper Gao

Hong dived the right way but couldn't get near it. Chastain ripped off her jersey and dropped to her knees, screaming in joy. Her celebration became one of the most famous in sports history. Meanwhile, the US team's performance brought unheard-of attention to women's sports, showing that soccer was not just for men anymore.

THE MIRACLE OF ISTANBUL

A joyous crowd of Liverpool fans arrived at Atatürk Olympic Stadium in Istanbul, Turkey, for the 2005 men's European Champions League final. Once the most powerful team in England, Liverpool was back in its first European final in 20 years. Despite Liverpool being an underdog against Italian giant AC Milan, fans of "the Reds" came in singing. However, they were soon laid low. AC Milan scored in the first minute of the game on its way to a 3–0 halftime lead.

Coming out for the second half, players were greeted by Liverpool fans belting out "You'll Never Walk Alone," the club's inspirational anthem. Liverpool captain Steven Gerrard responded with a perfectly placed header in the 54th minute to cut the deficit to 3–1. As he raced back to the center circle, Gerrard pumped his arms to encourage even more noise.

With its fans roaring, Liverpool scored two more goals in the next seven minutes. Suddenly, the game was tied 3–3. It stayed that way the rest of the half, forcing extra time.

With just three minutes to play, AC Milan's superstar striker Andriy Shevchenko powered a header on goal from close range. Liverpool's goalkeeper, Jerzy Dudek, knocked it into the ground. He then recovered in time to deflect Shevchenko's rebound chance over the crossbar. Dudek later called the moment, "The save of my career. Of my life."

Dudek wasn't finished. In the penalty shootout, his constant movement on the goal line distracted AC Milan's shooters. Milan's first kick went over the crossbar. Dudek

Jerzy Dudek's heroics in goal during the 2005 Champions League final helped Liverpool secure its fifth European title.

punched away the second. The shootout stood 3–2 Liverpool when Shevchenko stepped up as Milan's last chance. Dudek dived to his right. Shevchenko sent his shot down the middle. As Dudek's body flew toward the side, he reached his left arm back toward the ball. It slammed against his palm and bounced harmlessly to the grass. The "Miracle of Istanbul" was complete.

CHAPTER 2

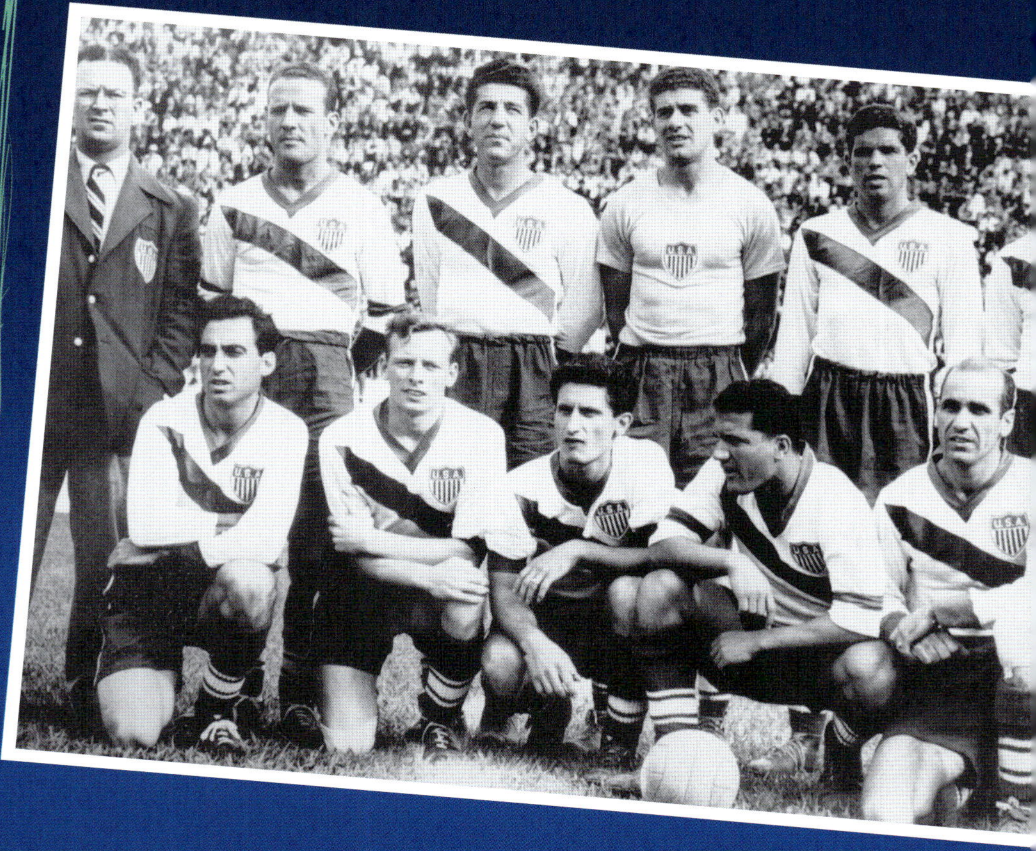

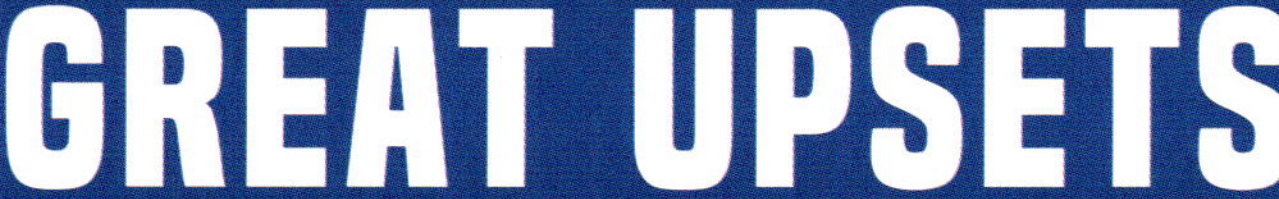

GREAT UPSETS

On paper, England versus the United States at the 1950 men's World Cup was an enormous mismatch. The English had invented modern soccer. Many believed the world's best players were English. In fact, English team officials thought so much of their team that they had refused to play in the

first three World Cups. Finally making its tournament debut, England expected to show up in Brazil and cruise to victory.

Meanwhile, people in the United States barely cared about soccer at the time. The national team was made up of semipro players and amateurs. The goalkeeper, Frank Borghi, drove a hearse in St. Louis. Midfielder Walter Bahr was a Philadelphia schoolteacher. Forward Joe Gaetjens was paying his way through school in New York by working as a dishwasher.

England had won its opening game 2–0 over Chile. The Americans fell 3–1 to Spain. Before the teams met for their second game on June 29 in Belo Horizonte, US coach Bill Jeffrey was quoted as saying, "We have no chance."

It looked as if England would crush the United States early. Borghi had to stop six shots in the first 12 minutes. But the score was still 0–0 in the 37th minute when Bahr attempted a long shot. The ball sailed through the air, then tipped off the diving Gaetjens's head, fooling English goalkeeper Bert Williams. The Americans were shockingly ahead 1–0.

Stunned, the English players turned up the pressure. For the rest of the match, they worked furiously to score the tying goal. But time after time, Borghi and the US team turned them away. In the end, Gaetjens's goal held up. The 1–0 shocker was complete.

The US players, *in white,* did everything they could to keep Thomas Finney, *center,* and England off the scoreboard.

When news of the result was sent back to the two countries, many were in disbelief. Some in England thought the 1–0 score was a misprint. They figured England had won 10–1. The *New York Times* didn't report the result, thinking it was fake.

The victory didn't help the United States much. The Americans fell to Chile in their third group stage game and were eliminated. And the country didn't return to the World Cup for another 40 years. But upsets can be some of the most stunning and memorable results in sports. Decades later, fans still remember the Americans' win over England in 1950 as one of the great upsets in soccer history.

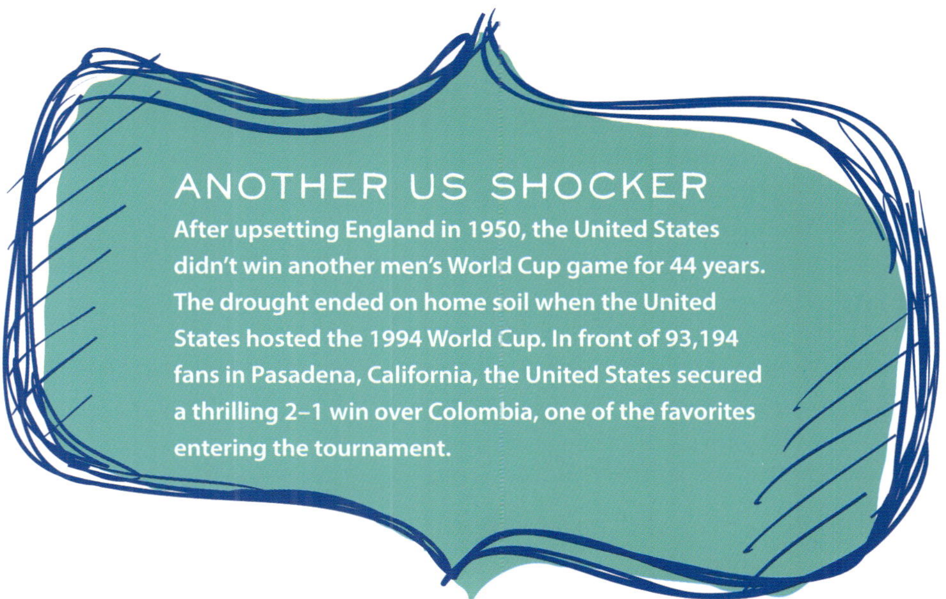

THE MIRACLE OF BERN

Entering the 1954 men's World Cup, Hungary had not lost a match in four years. Led by superstar forward Ferenc Puskás, one of the game's all-time great goal scorers, the "Mighty Magyars" had won the 1952 Olympics. Many expected the eastern European country to add its first World Cup title at the 1954 tournament in Switzerland.

True to form, Hungary rolled up 17 goals in its first two games. That included an 8–3 win over West Germany. So when the two teams met again for the title in the Swiss city of Bern, few expected a close game.

On a rainy night, Puskás opened the scoring in the sixth minute. Teammate Zoltán Czibor doubled the Magyars' lead two minutes later. But the West Germans quickly got one goal back. Then, in the 18th minute, Helmut Rahn poked in a corner kick to tie the game 2–2.

Stunned, the Hungarians responded with a flurry of chances as the game went on. One of Hungary's shots bounced off the post. A West German defender stopped another one on the goal line. All the while, West German goalkeeper Toni Turek made several excellent saves.

The game was still tied 2–2 with only minutes to play when a ball fell to Rahn outside the Hungary penalty area. The forward's low shot glided across the wet grass and past

Fans carry West German striker Franz Walter off the field following the 1954 World Cup final in Bern, Switzerland.

Hungarian goalkeeper Gyula Grosics. In the 84th minute, West Germany led 3–2.

The Hungarians did not go down quietly. Puskás thought he had scored three minutes later. However, his goal was waved off for being offside. As time ticked down, Turek made a diving save to keep the West Germans ahead. When the final whistle blew, "the Miracle of Bern" had ended the Hungarians' 31-match unbeaten streak.

Cameroon's François Omam-Biyik celebrates after scoring the go-ahead goal against Argentina in the 1990 World Cup.

THE INDOMITABLE LIONS ROAR

Entering the 1990 men's World Cup, African countries had never made much noise in the tournament. Cameroon was no different. The country had reached the tournament only once before, in 1982. It played three tie games and went home without advancing.

The 1990 World Cup was held in Italy. Cameroon was selected to play in the opening game against Argentina, the defending champion. The Argentines still had Diego Maradona, the world's best player. Hardly anyone expected a result other than an Argentina victory.

In a surprise, the game remained scoreless at halftime. However, Cameroon's chances weren't helped much when midfielder André Kana-Biyik stopped an Argentina break with a hard foul. He received a red card for the reckless challenge. The team known as the "Indomitable Lions" would have to play the remaining 30-plus minutes of the match with only 10 players.

Just six minutes later, Cameroon was awarded a free kick near the far sideline. A weak cross was deflected high into the air. François Omam-Biyik, whose brother had just been red-carded, met it just outside the six-yard box and sent a downward header toward the goal. Argentina goalkeeper Nery Pumpido fumbled it, and the ball dribbled into the net.

It wasn't a pretty goal, but winning ugly was fine with Cameroon. The team stuck to its plan of frustrating Argentina's attackers with physical defending. In the 88th minute, speedy Argentine forward Claudio Caniggia took off into the Cameroon half with the ball. One defender tried to take

him out but missed. But just after Caniggia danced past that challenge, he was drilled by defender Benjamin Massing. The collision was so violent that Massing's shoe came flying off. He had barely put it back on before he was shown a red card.

Even with nine players, Cameroon held on for the 1–0 win. It was the start of a thrilling run that reached the quarterfinals. At the time, it was the deepest an African team had ever advanced at the World Cup.

A BEACON OF HOPE

Coming into the 2011 Women's World Cup, few thought of Japan as a global soccer power. But this Japanese team was different. Four months before the tournament began in Germany, the northeast coast of Japan was hit with a devastating tsunami that killed more than 18,000 people. The national team hoped it could inspire its nation through its performance at the World Cup. That inspiration drove the Japanese all the way to the final against the United States.

The United States had long been a power in women's soccer. In 25 previous meetings between the two teams, Japan had never won. And hotshot American striker Alex Morgan put her team up 1–0 in the 69th minute. A record third World Cup title for the United States appeared likely. However, Japan midfielder Aya Miyama scored in the 81st minute. The whistle blew a few minutes later, sending the 1–1 game into extra time.

Any momentum Japan had gotten from Miyama's goal appeared to be lost in the 103rd minute. Morgan beat two Japanese defenders near the edge of the penalty area. Waiting on the top of the six-yard box was Abby Wambach. One of the game's all-time greatest scorers, the 5-foot-11 US striker had a knack for winning headers. And once again, she drove the ball into the net using her head. The Americans led 2–1.

It looked as if the United States had done enough to win. But Japan had Homare Sawa. Serving as team captain, the midfielder had been the best player at the tournament. She scored her tournament-high fourth goal in the semifinal to help Japan advance. Sawa then scored her fifth goal of the tournament in the 117th minute of the final, flicking a corner kick into the US net.

That forced a penalty shootout. Miyama scored Japan's first penalty while the first three American players missed. After Wambach buried her penalty, midfielder Saki Kumagai had a

Homare Sawa and Japan celebrate becoming the first Asian country to win a World Cup.

chance to win it for Japan. She rocketed her penalty into the top of the net. Months after unspeakable tragedy, Japan was on top of the world. And for the first time ever, an Asian team was a World Cup champion.

CHAPTER 3

LATE DRAMA

Bayern Munich and Manchester United each entered the 1999 men's European Champions League final with a chance to make history. Each team had won its country's league and most important cup competitions that year. Whichever team won the Champions League would

achieve what is called a "treble"—three major trophies in the same season.

The final was held at the famous Camp Nou stadium in Barcelona, Spain. In front of 90,245 fans, Bayern struck first. Less than six minutes into the game, the German champions earned a free kick. Midfielder Mario Basler knocked it in for a 1–0 lead. Bayern continued to control the match after that. The team might have built on its lead in the second half. However, two shots hit the post.

Looking for a spark, Manchester United manager Alex Ferguson turned to his bench. The English champions brought on striker Teddy Sheringham in the 67th minute. Still trailing in the 80th minute, Ferguson subbed on another attacker in Ole Gunnar Solskjær. But nothing seemed to work. Bayern still led 1–0 as the game entered stoppage time.

Now desperate, Manchester United threw everyone forward for a corner kick. Even goalkeeper Peter Schmeichel came up to join the attack. As players from both sides scrambled for the ball off the corner, it fell to Sheringham in the six-yard box. He turned and hit it with his right foot. The low, spinning shot slid into the corner of the net. Suddenly, in the first minute of stoppage time, the game was tied 1–1.

Extra time was looming. Then, two minutes later, United earned another corner. This time, Sheringham rose for a header at the near post. He headed it down and toward the far post. Solskjær lunged with his right toe and poked the ball into the net. No extra time was needed. Manchester United's late rally secured the team's first treble.

The Bayern players couldn't believe the result. "We dominated the game for 89 minutes," said veteran midfielder Lothar Matthäus. "It taught us that you only win a game if you are ahead at the final whistle."

Manchester United players mob Ole Gunnar Solskjær after his game-winning goal against Bayern Munich.

WAMBACH SAVES THE DAY

The US women's soccer team hadn't experienced many lows in its history entering the 2007 World Cup in China. Then Brazil walloped the Americans 4–0 in that year's semifinals. It was a humiliating defeat for the US players. To make matter worse, the teams were staying at the same hotel. And Brazil's players angered the US team by dancing in the lobby right in front of them.

Four years later, the Brazilians hoped to humiliate the US team once again when the teams met in the quarterfinals of the 2011 World Cup in Germany. The United States received a boost in the game's second minute when Brazilian defender Daiane deflected a ball into her own net. The Americans' 1–0 lead held until the second half. Then disaster struck for the United States. Marta, Brazil's all-world striker, drove into the penalty area. US defender Rachel Buehler took her down hard. Buehler earned a red card for her play, and Marta scored her penalty to tie the match. Still tied 1–1 after 90 minutes, the game went into extra time.

The United States had never fallen short of the semifinals at a major global tournament. Marta and her teammates were determined to change that. Two minutes into extra time, Marta scored again to put Brazil in the lead. Already down a player due to Buehler's red card, the Americans scrambled to mount a comeback. But with stoppage time starting on the second extra time session, they still trailed 2–1.

With just seconds left to play, US winger Megan Rapinoe brought the ball up the left wing. A swift kick sent a long, desperate cross into the Brazil penalty area. Racing to the other end of the cross was teammate Abby Wambach. The towering striker outjumped a defender and the goalkeeper. Wambach's powerful header rippled the net to tie the game.

The 122nd-minute strike was the latest goal ever scored at either the women's or men's World Cup. But the United States still had to win the penalty shootout. Brazil's third shooter was Daiane. She fired a shot to US goalkeeper Hope Solo's right. Solo lunged and knocked it away. Brazil's goalie was unable to match that. All five American shooters scored to send the US on to the semifinals once again.

Abby Wambach scores her unlikely 122nd-minute goal against Brazil to keep the United States alive in the 2011 Women's World Cup.

MANCHESTER MIRACLE

England's Premier League celebrated its 20th season in 2011–12. Most of those seasons had been dominated by one club. Manchester United already had 12 Premier League titles, including the season before. Meanwhile, United's local rival, Manchester City, was mostly mediocre. However, after new ownership took over in 2008, "the Citizens" began inching their way toward contending. And entering the final day of the 2011–12 season, the two teams were neck and neck for the title.

The teams were even on points. But Manchester City had outscored its opponents by a higher margin over the course of the season. That gave City the tiebreaker. So if both teams finished the season with the same result, City would claim the league title. To heighten the drama on the final match day, all 10 Premier League matches kicked off at the same time. Manchester City was hosting Queens Park Rangers (QPR). Manchester United was away at Sunderland. Fans of both teams kept one eye on the other's game all afternoon.

City entered stoppage time trailing 2–1, a result that would all but guarantee United another title. Just then, City striker Edin Džeko scored on a header to tie the game. As the City fans nervously celebrated, news spread that Manchester United's match had ended. The Red Devils had won 1–0. If those results held, United would win the title.

Manchester City's Sergio Aguero prepares to rip the game-winning shot against Queens Park Rangers in their 2012 Premier League finale.

United's players stayed on the field at Sunderland, waiting to be presented the trophy. But there was still time to play in Manchester. City threw everyone forward. Striker Sergio Aguero passed the ball to Mario Balotelli at the edge of the penalty area. Falling backward, Balotelli poked out a return pass for Aguero. The Argentine controlled the ball and skipped past a defender. He then rifled the winning shot into the QPR net with just seconds remaining.

The fans at City's Etihad Stadium erupted. Aguero ripped off his jersey and swung it around his head as he sprinted around the field. In Sunderland, Manchester United's players were stunned. It was City's first title in England's top division since 1967–68. And it was one of the most unbelievable moments in the country's long, storied soccer history.

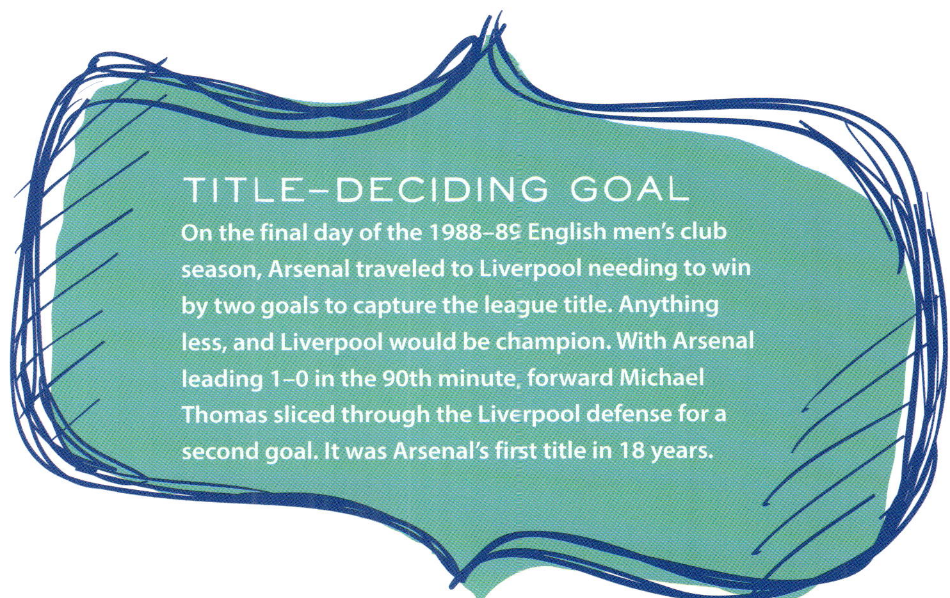

BALED OUT

Major League Soccer (MLS) has produced many heart-stopping moments over the years. But the 2022 MLS Cup between Los Angeles Football Club (LAFC) and the Philadelphia Union proved to be perhaps the most intense in the championship game's 27-year history.

The teams came into the final with the league's best records that season. And after 80 minutes, they were deadlocked at 1–1. Then the drama really started to pick up. LAFC defender Jesús David Murillo scored off a corner in the 83rd minute. The game was being played in the team's home stadium. But before the crowd could get too excited, Philadelphia's Jack Elliott headed the ball into the goal off a free kick two minutes later.

The score remained 2–2 in the 116th minute when LAFC goalkeeper Maxime Crépeau and Union substitute Cory Burke chased after a loose ball. The players collided. Not only did Crépeau receive a red card, but he was also injured on the play. The long delay for his treatment created nine minutes of stoppage time. Elliott took advantage, scoring in the 124th minute to put the Union ahead. LAFC would need a miracle.

Alas, the California team had a secret weapon. For most of the 2010s, Gareth Bale had been one of the sport's most dangerous attacking players while starring for Real Madrid in Spain. The Welshman had joined LAFC during that 2022 season.

Gareth Bale, *in black*, scores a game-tying goal to keep LAFC alive against the Philadelphia Union in the 2022 MLS Cup.

Injuries had slowed the 33-year-old. But in extra time, LAFC subbed him in. And in the 128th minute, Bale locked on to a cross and headed home another tying goal. The crowd was still roaring when the teams went to a shootout.

John McCarthy had come in to replace Crépeau in goal. LAFC held a 1–0 lead in the shootout when the substitute goalkeeper stuffed Philadelphia midfielder José Martinez's attempt. McCarthy then cemented his legend by stopping the next shot as well. LAFC won the shootout 3–0. Though he had played less than 13 minutes of the marathon game, McCarthy was named the contest's Most Valuable Player as LAFC claimed its first league title.

CHAPTER 4

ICONIC
PERFORMANCES

The more than 96,000 fans packed inside Wembley Stadium in London, England, started fearing the worst. England's men had reached the 1966 World Cup final. But just 12 minutes into the game, West Germany forward Helmut Haller scored to put his team up 1–0.

This was England's fifth attempt at winning a World Cup. Fans believed this group, competing at home, really had a chance to win the country's first championship. Now, however, those chances were looking bleak.

England forward Geoff Hurst helped settle the nerves of the hometown crowd. His header off a free kick tied the game for England just six minutes after it fell behind. England's Martin Peters added another goal late in the second half. But West Germany tied the score just before the 90th minute to force extra time.

GERMAN RUTHLESSNESS

At the 2014 men's World Cup, host Brazil faced Germany in the semifinals. What many Brazilians hoped would be a dream come true turned into a nightmare. By halftime the Germans led 5–0. In one of the most dominant team performances in World Cup history, Germany cruised to the final with a 7–1 victory.

In the 101st minute, Hurst controlled a pass with his back to the West German goal. As he spun, Hurst unleashed a powerful shot. It bounced off the crossbar and fell straight down before spinning back into the field. No one knew whether the ball had gone in. The referee checked with his assistant on the sideline, then awarded the goal. To this day, it is one of the most disputed goals in World Cup history.

Despite the controversy, England led 3–2. And the jubilant fans at Wembley started to spill onto the field in the game's final seconds. Some players stopped playing, thinking that the game was over.

However, it was not. Soon Hurst found himself on a breakaway. It ended when he hammered a left-footed shot high into the West German net to seal the 4–2 win. It was the first hat trick ever in a World Cup final.

Teammates lift captain Bobby Moore into the air in celebration of England's 1966 World Cup championship.

And England, the country that had invented the sport, was finally on top of the soccer world.

THE MAGIC OF MARADONA

Tension between Argentina and England existed long before their quarterfinal meeting at the 1986 men's World Cup. The countries had met in a brutal match 20 years earlier at the 1966 tournament. Political disputes in the years that followed only inflamed the relationship. Then Argentina's star player, Diego Maradona, turned up the heat even more.

The two rivals met again in the quarterfinals of the 1986 World Cup in Mexico. Neither team scored through the first 50 minutes. Then, in the 51st minute, a looping ball came into the England penalty area. Peter Shilton, the team's 6-foot goalkeeper, came out to grab it. But the 5-foot-5-inch Maradona beat him to the ball. The Argentine attacker popped it into the net to put his team up 1–0. Almost immediately, the England players started screaming at the referee. They claimed Maradona had used his hand, not his head, to score. But the protests didn't work. Argentina's lead held.

Five minutes later, Maradona controlled the ball just inside his own half. He took off toward the England goal. On his way, he juked past five English defenders. Some were trying to slow him down. Others were simply trying to foul Maradona. But nothing could stop the hard-charging attacker. After his long run, he dribbled past Shilton and scored into an open net to make it 2–0.

England defenders can only chase as Diego Maradona races toward his "Goal of the Century" for Argentina in the 1986 World Cup.

Though England scored late, Argentina held on to win 2–1. Maradona was asked after the match about his controversial first goal. "A little with the head of Maradona and a little with the hand of God" was his reply. The play is now known as the "Hand of God" goal. Maradona's second goal is now called the "Goal of the Century." Argentina went on to win the World Cup, and Maradona's play against England became the defining performance of his career.

LLOYD LIGHTS IT UP

Big moments never seemed to faze American forward Carli Lloyd. A famously intense player, she scored the goals that secured the US women Olympic gold medals in 2008 and 2012. However, on the biggest stage in 2011, she had fallen short. Facing Japan in the Women's World Cup final, Lloyd missed her attempt in the penalty shootout. Japan went on to win the game and the championship.

Four years later, the teams met again in the 2015 World Cup final in Vancouver, Canada. This time, Lloyd was determined to leave with the trophy. It didn't take her long to show it. Just three minutes into the game, the Americans had a corner kick. Megan Rapinoe swung in a hard, low ball. Lloyd began her run from well outside the penalty area. She then outraced the defenders and poked the ball into the net with her left foot.

Less than three minutes later, US midfielder Lauren Holiday took a free kick from the right side. The low ball bounced off several players in the box. In the scramble, Lloyd broke free and knocked it in from close range.

The United States went up 3–0 in the 14th minute on a goal by Holiday. And two minutes later, Lloyd took advantage of the stunned Japanese players. As she picked up the ball near midfield, Lloyd spotted Japan goalkeeper Ayumi Kaihori well off her goal line. In a daring move, Lloyd unleashed a long looping shot. Kaihori scrambled back. She could only get a finger on the ball as it sailed in.

Carli Lloyd celebrates her third goal of the 2015 Women's World Cup final against Japan. The United States dominated to win 5–2.

Lloyd's final goal was nominated for the Puskás Award. That is given to the scorer of the most beautiful goal of each year. More importantly, Lloyd's brilliance led the United States to a 5–2 win. That gave the United States its first World Cup title since 1999. And Lloyd became the first woman to ever score a hat trick in a World Cup final.

MESSI VS. MBAPPÉ

Lionel Messi had won just about every major championship in his historic career. The one trophy missing, however, was the biggest of them all. The 2022 men's World Cup was Messi's fifth with Argentina. As the tournament played out in Qatar, the 35-year-old forward looked like a player determined to finally claim a world title.

Just when an opponent thought it had Messi contained, the 5-foot-6 superstar seemed to find an opening. Through six games, Messi had scored five goals. He needed just one more win to become a World Cup champion.

Standing in Argentina's path, however, was France. The defending champion was loaded with talent. And no player shone brighter than Kylian Mbappé. The speedy winger had been one of the breakout stars on France's 2018 championship team as a teenager. Now going into the 2022 final, he had matched Messi with five goals.

The 2022 World Cup final was as much a battle between Argentina and France as it was a showdown between the teams' two superstars, Lionel Messi, *left*, and Kylian Mbappé.

Many in the stadium wanted to see Messi win a World Cup for the first time. They were delighted when he scored on a first-half penalty kick. Teammate Ángel Di María doubled the lead to 2–0 soon after. And as the clock wound toward 80 minutes, Argentina appeared on its way to an easy win. That's when Mbappé took over.

He cut the lead in half with a penalty kick goal in the 80th minute. Then, just a minute later, he connected on a superb volley to tie the game at 2–2. Just like that, the game was on.

Some players shrink under pressure. The moment only seemed to motivate Messi and Mbappé. In extra time, Messi

broke through. In the 108th minute, he pounced on a rebound to put Argentina up 3–2. But just 10 minutes later, a handball in the Argentina box set up a France penalty kick. Mbappé smashed it into the net. With that, he joined Hurst and Lloyd as hat trick scorers in World Cup finals.

The breathtaking game wasn't over. Mbappé stepped up first for France in the penalty shootout. And the 23-year-old calmly drove the ball past Argentina's diving goalie. Now it was Messi's turn. The Argentine approached the penalty spot. Just before shooting, Messi paused. When French goalie Hugo Lloris started to move left, Messi slowly rolled the ball the other direction. Lloris tried to reverse and dive back on the ball, but he was too late.

The two superstars had done their jobs. Now it was up to their teammates. Defender Gonzalo Montiel shot fourth for Argentina. With his team needing just one more goal for the win, he calmly buried a shot into the lower left corner. Argentina had won, but so too had the fans. On the biggest stage, Messi finally claimed soccer's biggest prize. And Mbappé, it was clear, was the sport's next great star.

GLOSSARY

CAPTAIN
A team's leader on the field.

CROSS
A pass delivered from the side of the field toward the middle.

EXTRA TIME
Two 15-minute periods added to a game if the score is tied at the end of regulation.

FREE KICK
An unguarded kick awarded to a team after an opponent's foul.

HAT TRICK
Three or more goals by the same player in one game.

INDOMITABLE
Impossible to defeat.

KNOCKOUT
Games within a tournament in which the losing team is eliminated.

PENALTY AREA
The box in front of the goal where a player is granted a penalty kick if he or she is fouled.

PENALTY SHOOTOUT
A series of penalty kicks held after extra time to determine the winner of a game.

REBOUND
A loose ball that remains in play after a goalie makes a save.

RED CARD
A punishment given to a player, usually for violent conduct or dangerous play, that ejects that player from the game.

SEMIPRO
Someone who is paid for doing something but not paid enough to earn a living.

STOPPAGE TIME
Also known as injury time, a number of minutes tacked onto the end of a half for stoppages that occurred during play from injuries, free kicks, and goals.

VOLLEY
A ball that is kicked out of the air rather than off the ground.

MORE INFORMATION

BOOKS

Hewson, Anthony K. *GOATs of Soccer.* Minneapolis, MN: Abdo Publishing, 2022.

Jökulsson, Illugi. *Stars of World Soccer.* New York: Abbeville Press, 2020.

Shaw, Gina. *What is the Women's World Cup?* New York: Penguin Workshop, 2023.

ONLINE RESOURCES

To learn more about the best soccer matches, please visit abdobooklinks.com or scan this QR code. These links are routinely monitored and updated to provide the most current information available.

INDEX

ABOUT THE AUTHOR

Luke Hanlon is a sportswriter and editor based in Minneapolis.